HEALTH&
the Body

Healthy
Lifestyles

BY GEMMA MᶜMULLEN

©2017
Book Life
King's Lynn
Norfolk PE30 4LS

ISBN: 978-1-78637-094-5

Written by:
Gemma McMullen

Edited by:
Grace Jones

Designed by:
Natalie Carr

LOOK FOR THE WORDS LIKE **THIS** IN THE GLOSSARY ON PAGE 31.

ISLINGTON

12116

29 MAR 2017

-9 MAY 2019

Islington Libraries

020 7527 6900   www.islington.gov.uk/libraries

Contents

4 HEALTHY LIVING

6 THE HUMAN BODY

8 THE BRAIN

10 THE HEART

12 THE LUNGS

14 THE DIGESTIVE SYSTEM

18 THE OTHER ORGANS

22 THE SKIN

24 THE SKELETON

26 THE MUSCLES

28 THE SENSES

31 GLOSSARY

32 INDEX

WHERE DOES YOUR FOOD GO?

FIND OUT INSIDE ON PAGE 14

HOW MANY SENSES DO YOU HAVE?

FEATURED ON PAGE 28

HEALTHY

HEALTHY BODY

The way that we treat our bodies is extremely important because without good health we would **CEASE** to exist. The food that we eat and the amount that we exercise both contribute massively to the health of our bodies. We need to respect our bodies so that they stay healthy for longer.

WHAT IS HEALTHY LIVING?

ALTHOUGH WE ARE ALL UNIQUE, OUR BODIES ALL WORK IN THE SAME WAY AND NEED THE SAME THINGS TO STAY HEALTHY.

HEALTHY living is the term given to the ideal way of living our lives; put simply, it means that we live our lives in the healthiest way possible. Healthy living relates to every single aspect of our lives, from the things that we eat to the amount that we sleep.

Living

HEALTHY CHOICES

Whilst it is unlikely that a person will always choose the healthiest option, it is important that we take all options into consideration so that we are able to make **INFORMED CHOICES** about the way that we live our lives. This book is about the human body and the ways to keep it healthy.

HEALTHY MIND

The health of our minds is of equal importance to that of our bodies. Our minds control the way that we think and the ways in which we use our bodies. Keeping a healthy mind includes having healthy relationships with others and being able to deal with our problems rationally.

THE HUMAN

BEING HUMAN

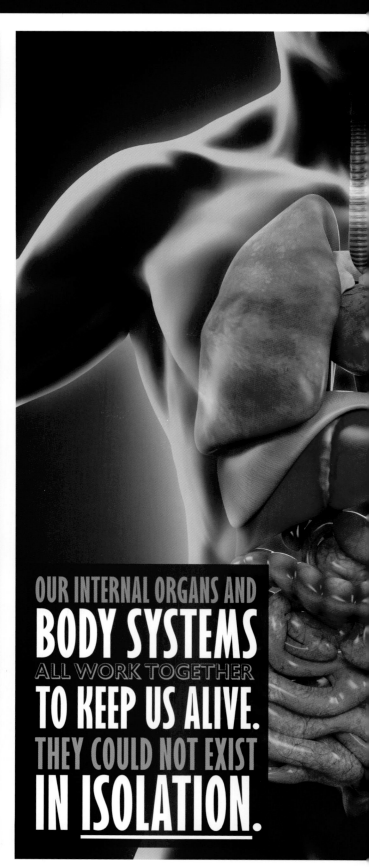

HUMAN beings are a species of animal. Humans have bodies made up of body parts which all work together so that we can think, move and grow. No two humans look exactly the same or have the same personalities, but our bodies all need the same things and all work in the same way.

BODY SYSTEMS

Humans are the most intelligent creatures on planet Earth and have long been studying how the human body works. Although we all look different on the outside, human beings all look almost identical on the inside. We are all made up of organs and bodily systems that work together.

OUR INTERNAL ORGANS AND **BODY SYSTEMS** ALL WORK TOGETHER **TO KEEP US ALIVE.** THEY COULD NOT EXIST **IN ISOLATION.**

Body

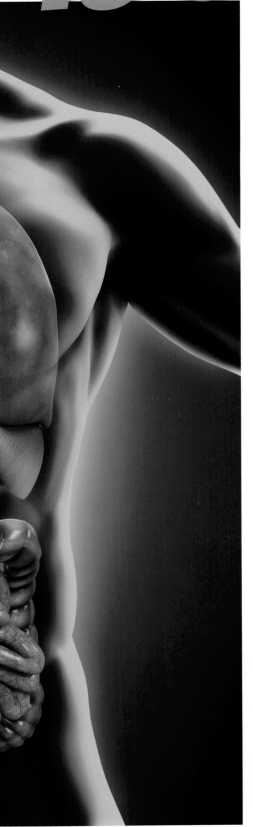

ADAPTABILITY

Whilst human bodies all work in the same way, they are able to adapt to a huge variety of living conditions. The Inuit people, for example, have adapted their lifestyles to suit very cold and icy conditions, whilst other humans live in hot deserts and rainforests. In a similar way, some people choose to live a more fast-paced lifestyle in busy cities, whereas other people prefer the slower pace of a rural lifestyle.

BODY SHAPE

Whilst all bodies are the same, the way that we treat them can effect how well they work. It is important to keep your body in good shape by eating well and exercising the right amount. The better you treat your body, the more likely you are to live a long, healthy life.

HUMANS LIVE ON SIX OF THE SEVEN CONTINENTS OF THE WORLD.

THE Brain

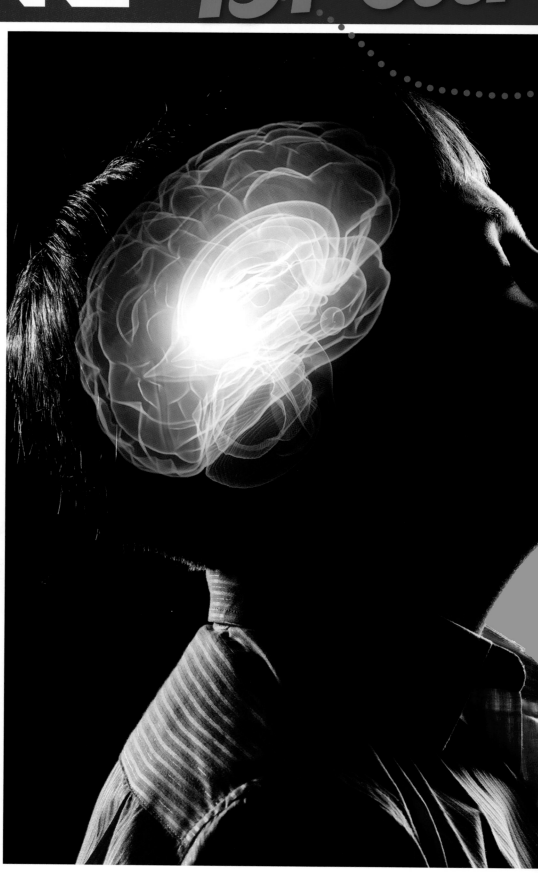

THE NERVES

Nerves run from the brain to all parts of the body. When we move, it is because the brain has sent messages along the nerves to the parts of the body needed for the action. This process happens so quickly that the message is sent **SUBCONSCIOUSLY**; we don't even need to think about doing it.

THIS DIAGRAM ILLUSTRATES THE NERVOUS SYSTEM, WHICH DELIVERS MESSAGES FROM THE BRAIN.

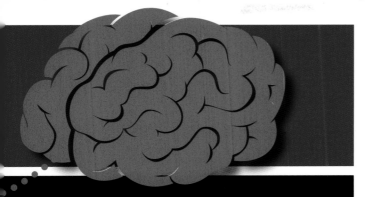

BRAIN POWER

THE brain is the most complex organ in the human body. It is the part of the body with which you learn and it controls everything that you do. It is located in the head and is protected by the skull.

OUR BRAINS STORE ALL OF THE INFORMATION THAT WE NEED TO DO THE THINGS WE DO, INCLUDING READING THIS BOOK!

LEARNING

From the day we were born, we have been learning to do new things and we will always continue to do so. When we start doing something new, it usually takes a while for our brains to remember how to do it without thinking, this includes physical activities like playing football. Our brains learn how to make our feet kick the ball correctly and run to the correct places on the pitch. They also allow us to remember the rules of the game. Once we have been playing football for a while, we start being able to play without having to think too much about what we are doing.

THE BRAIN SENDS MESSAGES TO YOUR FEET SO YOU ARE ABLE TO KICK THE BALL.

THE Heart

LEFT PUMP

RIGHT PUMP

TWO HALVES MAKE A WHOLE

The heart is split into two sides – the left side and the right side. The left side of the heart pushes blood that is filled with oxygen all around your body. It sends the blood via **VESSELS** called arteries. Once all of the oxygen has been taken from the blood, the blood returns to the right side of the heart, through vessels called veins, so that it can be oxygenated again.

POWERFUL MUSCLE

THE heart is a very strong muscle which is located in the chest. It is an extremely reliable muscle, which it needs to be – your life depends on it! The job of the heart is to pump blood around your body. It works very closely with the lungs.

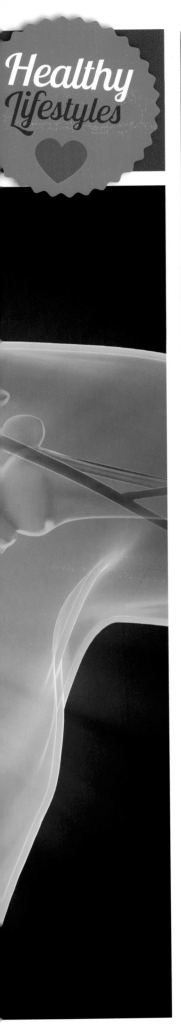

THE PULSE

When the heart pumps blood, the arteries expand a little. You can feel this at certain places on your body: the wrists and the neck are usually best. We call this a pulse.

By feeling your pulse, you will know how fast your heart is beating. You can count the beats to know how many times your heart beats each minute. Why not take your pulse when you are resting and then try again after exercise?

YEARS AGO, IT WAS BELIEVED THAT LOVE WAS GENERATED IN THE HEART, BUT WE NOW KNOW IT IS THE BRAIN THAT CONTROLS EMOTIONS.

A CHANGE OF PACE

The harder your body works, the quicker it uses the oxygen in your blood. For that reason, while you are exercising the heart beats faster and while you are resting it beats more slowly. You can check your heart rate by feeling your pulse.

THE Lungs

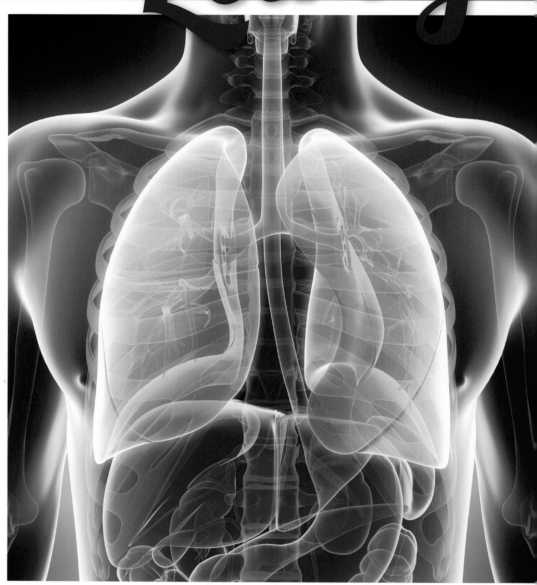

WHAT ARE LUNGS?

THE lungs are fairly large organs which sit in our chests. They work closely with the heart and are located next to it. The lungs and the heart are protected by the ribs of the skeleton. Human beings each have two lungs, both of which have the same function. The lungs are spongy and pink. They contain millions of tiny air sacs called alveoli.

BREATHING IN

Oxygen enters our bodies through either our nose or our mouth. It travels down our windpipes and into our lungs. In the lungs, the oxygen passes into our blood and the heart pumps it to where it is needed around the body (see previous page). We call breathing in 'inhaling'.

THE LEFT LUNG

IS A BIT SMALLER THAN THE **RIGHT LUNG: THE EXTRA SPACE IS NEEDED** TO ACCOMMODATE THE HEART.

MUSCLES

Oxygen is a gas that is found in the air. The human body needs oxygen to live. The lungs in our chests receive the oxygen from the air. The lungs are unable to move by themselves, so they rely on the muscles around them to inflate and deflate them. The diaphragm is one of the main muscles used to move the lungs.

THE DIAPHRAGM
IS A LARGE MUSCLE
WHICH SITS
UNDERNEATH
THE LUNGS.

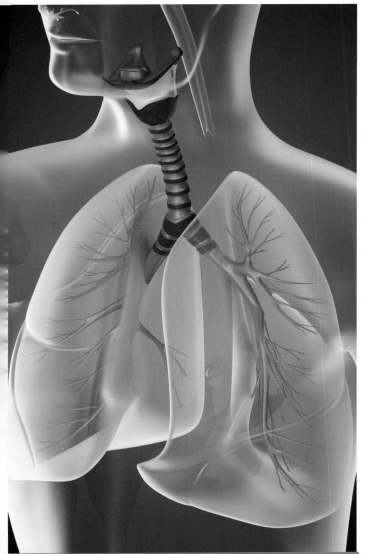

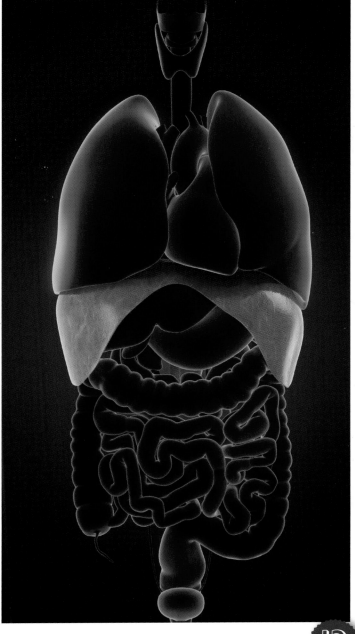

BREATHING OUT

When we exhale (breathe out), we are pushing stale air out of our bodies. The stale air contains a waste product called carbon dioxide. Carbon dioxide is a gas which our bodies cannot use.

THE DIGESTIVE

THE JOURNEY OF OUR FOOD

OUR bodies are designed to take in food – it is how we stay alive. Food enters our bodies through our mouths. It then makes its way through our bodies, being broken into tiny pieces and used as the body needs. We call the body parts responsible for this the digestive system.

SMELL AND TASTE

Our senses of smell and taste help to protect us. If a food does not smell nice, you are unlikely to put it into your mouth. If you do put something into your mouth which is foul-tasting, you still have time to spit it out. Smell and taste also help to start the digestive process. If you smell something delicious, your mouth starts to produce a clear liquid called saliva. Saliva makes your food moist and easier to eat.

THERE ARE THOUSANDS OF TASTE BUDS ON YOUR TONGUE WHICH DETECT FLAVOUR.

System

When your teeth and saliva have broken down the food in your mouth enough, you swallow it. The tube at the back of your mouth is called the oesophagus. The walls of the oesophagus are lined with muscles which help to push the food down into the stomach.

THE TONGUE IS A POWERFUL MUSCLE WHICH MOVES FOOD AROUND YOUR MOUTH, HELPING TO BREAK IT DOWN.

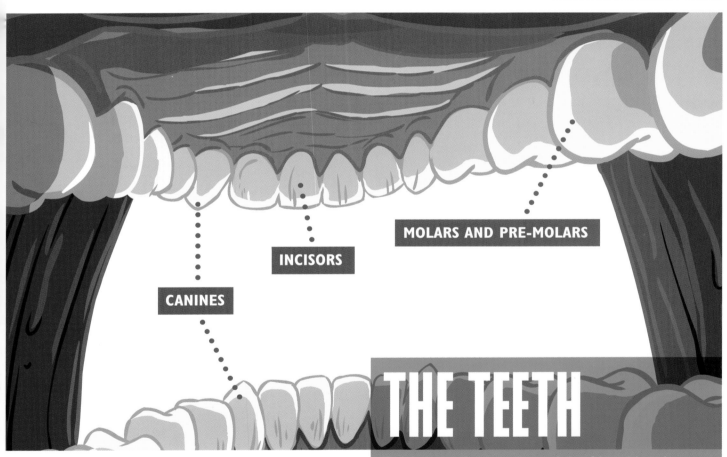

MOLARS AND PRE-MOLARS

INCISORS

CANINES

THE TEETH

WE ALSO BREATHE THROUGH OUR MOUTHS.

Teeth have the important job of breaking down your food into manageable sizes. The teeth at the front of your mouth (the incisors) are designed for biting, whilst the teeth at the back of the mouth (the molars and pre-molars) are designed for chewing. Canines are the sharpest teeth and they help to tear food such as meat.

1 THE STOMACH

FOOD that has been swallowed arrives at the stomach. The stomach is like an **ELASTICATED** bag for holding food. The stomach is a small organ, but it can stretch to accommodate a large amount of food. The muscles in the stomach **CHURN** the food and the strong acid in the stomach helps to break it down further.

2 THE SMALL INTESTINE

Once the food leaves the stomach, it enters the small intestine. The food is broken down even more and organs, such as the liver and pancreas, help to digest it. After as much as ten hours, the food is finally broken down enough to be absorbed by the body.

THE SMALL INTESTINE OF AN ADULT HUMAN CAN BE AS LONG AS 7.5 METERS

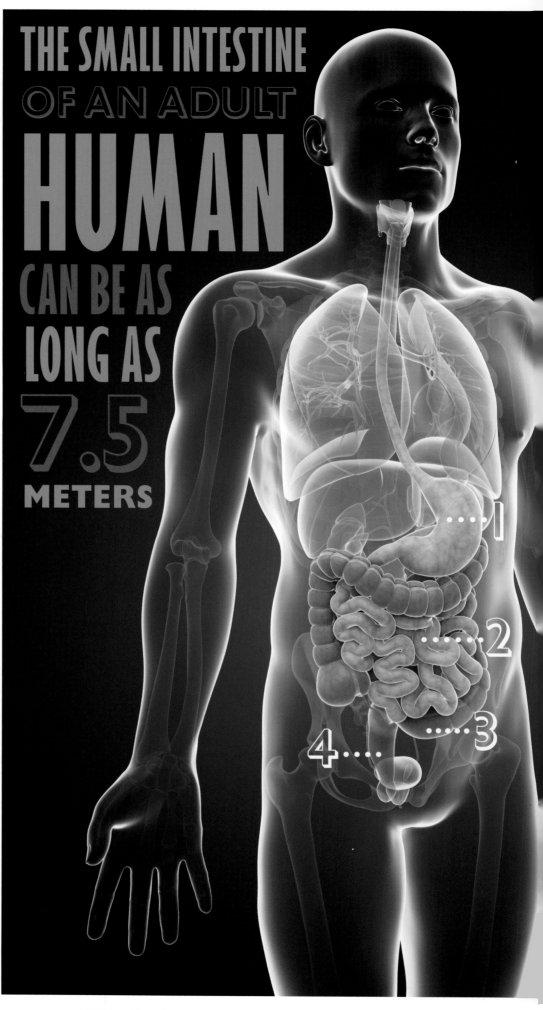

....1

.....2

.....3

4.....

3 THE LARGE INTESTINE

The food travels from the small intestine into the large intestine. The large intestine is much larger in **DIAMETER** than the small intestine, but it is nowhere near as long. The job of the large intestine is to absorb water from the remainder of the food. By the time the food has finished moving through the large intestine, it is more solid.

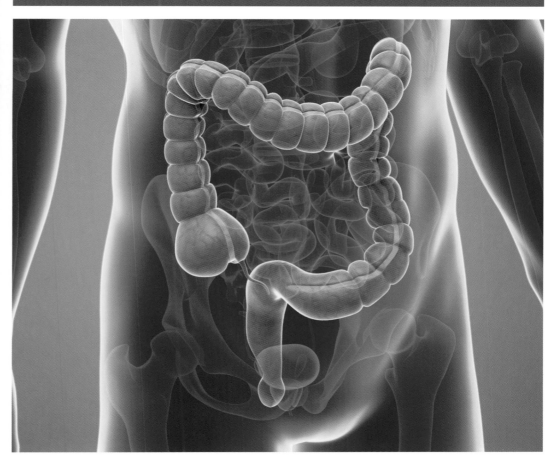

IT TAKES FOOD BETWEEN 18 AND 36 HOURS TO TRAVEL RIGHT THROUGH THE BODY AND EXIT AS WASTE.

4 WASTE PRODUCTS

The solid mass that remains once the food has travelled through the body is not needed. It waits at the end of the large intestine (the rectum) until you go to the toilet. This waste product is called faeces.

THE OTHER

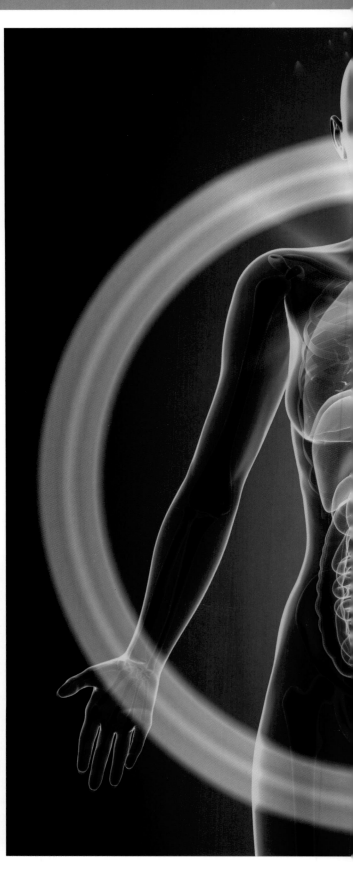

WHERE ARE THEY?

There are other organs in our bodies that also have important functions. Our organs are mostly found in the torso, rather than in our limbs (arms and legs). This means that if something happens to one of our limbs, our bodies will still survive.

SOMEBODY WHO CHOOSES TO ALLOW THEIR HEALTHY ORGANS TO BE USED FOR TRANSPLANTS IS CALLED A DONOR.

CAN WE LIVE WITHOUT THEM?

MOST of the organs in our bodies are needed for us to live and we would not be able to survive without them. The brain, heart and liver are all organs which humans must have. Some organs, such as the kidneys, come in pairs and it is possible for us to survive with only one of them. With the help of scientists, doctors are now able to transplant almost all working organs from one human to another.

Organs

THE LIVER

The liver has many important jobs to do. Perhaps the most important is that it cleans the blood and removes harmful substances called toxins, which occur when **PROTEINS** are broken down. The liver also makes bile, which is a digestive juice needed to break down and absorb fat into the body. The liver stores glycogen, a sugar made by breaking down carbohydrates, which is used by the cells in your body.

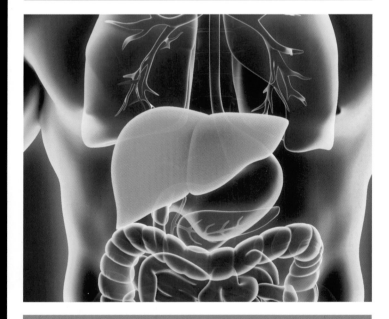

WHAT ELSE DOES THE LIVER DO?

There are even more jobs that this important organ performs. It has a part in making **CHOLESTEROL**, which our bodies need. The liver also helps our blood to clot, which is the process that eventually stops the bleeding when we have a cut. On top of this, when you take medicine, it is the liver that breaks it down and uses the ingredients to make you feel better.

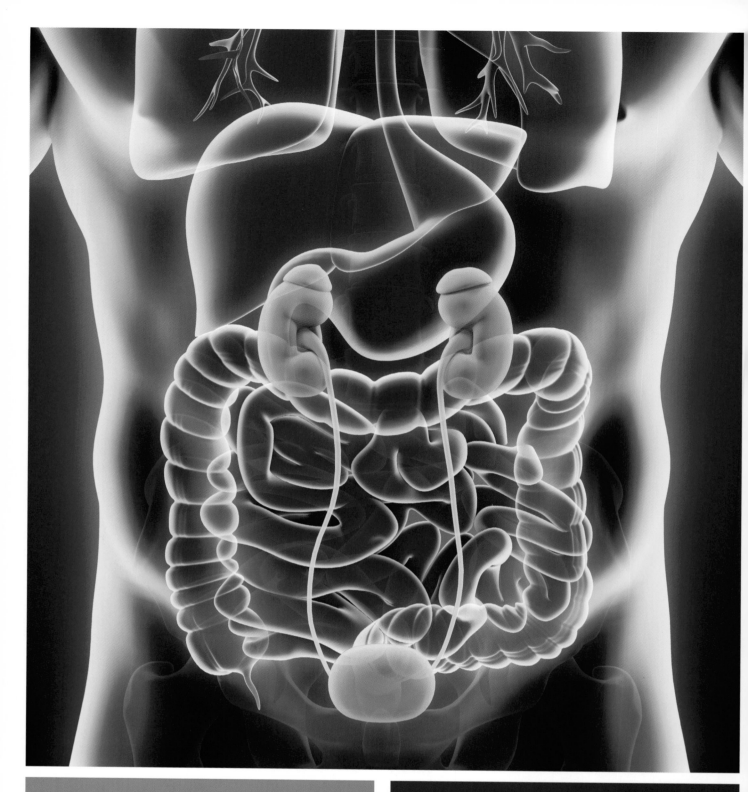

THE KIDNEYS

Humans each have two kidneys, though we can survive with just one. The main job of the kidneys is to filter organic waste out of the blood. Your kidneys filter your blood about 400 times every day! The waste that they collect mixes with water to make urine. The kidneys form part of the urinary system.

THE BLADDER

The bladder is connected to the kidneys by tubes called ureters. When urine is made by the kidneys, it travels down the ureters and is kept in the bladder. The bladder is like a storage sac. When your bladder is about half full, your brain sends a message to tell you to go to the toilet. Urine leaves your bladder via a tube called the urethra and exits the body.

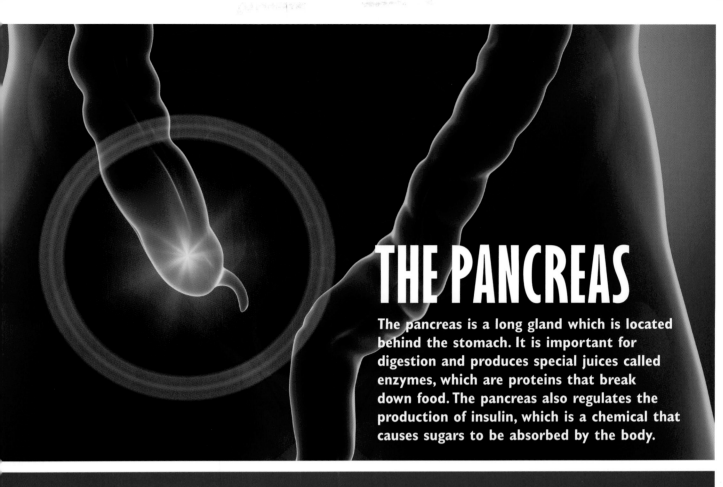

THE PANCREAS

The pancreas is a long gland which is located behind the stomach. It is important for digestion and produces special juices called enzymes, which are proteins that break down food. The pancreas also regulates the production of insulin, which is a chemical that causes sugars to be absorbed by the body.

THE APPENDIX

The appendix is a pouch that is attached to the large intestine. Unusually, scientists are unsure what the function of this organ actually is, although some think that it might be linked to our immune systems. Humans are able to live without their appendix. If the appendix gets infected, which is called an appendicitis, the appendix is removed via surgery.

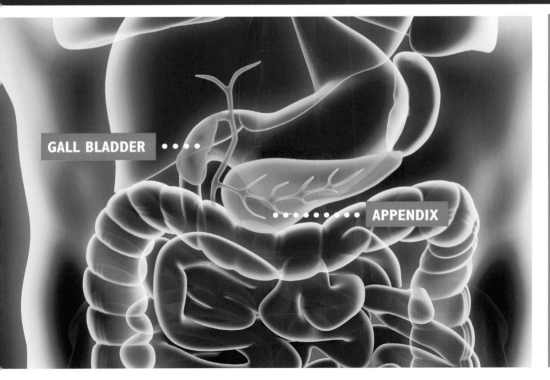

GALL BLADDER

APPENDIX

THE GALL BLADDER

The gall bladder is also part of the digestive system and helps to break down our food. We are able to live without our gall bladders and sometimes they are removed for medical reasons.

THE Skin!

THE EPIDERMIS

THE skin is the human body's largest organ. It covers the whole of your body and its main function is to protect. The skin is made up of layers and it continually replaces itself. The outer layer is called the epidermis. The epidermis keeps out substances, such as water and germs, and harmful rays from the sun. It also gives us the sense of touch.

THE EPIDERMIS · · · · ·

· · · · · · · · · · THE DERMIS

THE DERMIS

Beneath the epidermis is a thicker layer called the dermis. The dermis is filled with nerves and blood vessels. It helps to regulate the body's temperature by producing sweat in warm conditions. It also houses hair and nail **FOLLICLES,** which grow through the epidermis and offer further protection.

THE SKIN OF A FULLY GROWN ADULT WEIGHS AROUND 5KGS!

EVEN PEOPLE WITH DARK SKIN NEED TO BE CAREFUL TO LOOK AFTER THEIR SKIN IN THE SUN.

SKIN COLOUR

The colour of our skin is determined by a **PIGMENT** called melanin. Melanin is designed to protect our skin from burning in the sun. People from hot countries often have more melanin in their skins than people from cooler countries, because they need more protection. That is why people who **ORIGINATE** from hot countries often have darker skin than those who do not.

AS FINGERPRINTS ARE UNIQUE, POLICE ARE ABLE TO USE THEM TO PROVE WHETHER SOMEBODY WAS AT A CRIME SCENE.

FINGERPRINTS

The skin covering our hands is folded into tiny ridges. The purpose of the ridges is to help the skin to grip. The ridges form patterns of arches and loops. When a person touches something, tiny sweat prints of these patterns are left behind. We call these fingerprints. No two humans have the same fingerprints.

THE Skeleton

THEM BONES

THE skeleton is the frame that gives humans shape, supports the body and allows it to move. Some of the bones in the skeleton also offer protection to the internal organs. An adult skeleton is made up of 206 bones and is accountable for around one fifth of the body's total weight.

A BABY'S SKELETON HAS AROUND 300 BONES BUT THESE FUSE TOGETHER AS THEY GROW.

BONES AND JOINTS

When a baby is born, its bones are soft and flexible. As a child grows, the bones become harder. Adult bones are hard on the outside and soft in the middle. If a bone gets broken, it can repair itself over time. The bones in the skeleton fit together using joints. Most of the joints allow for movement.

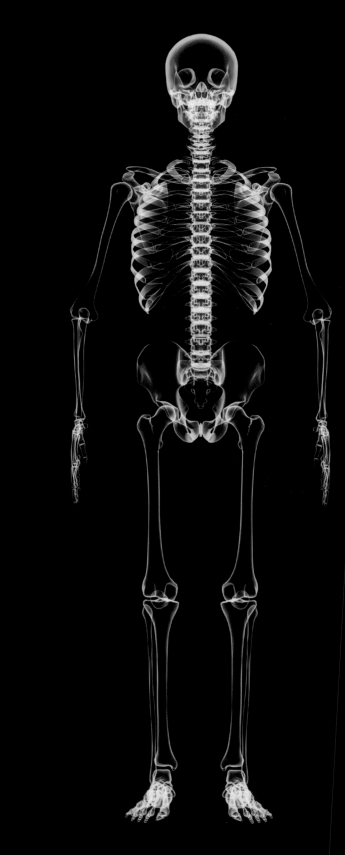

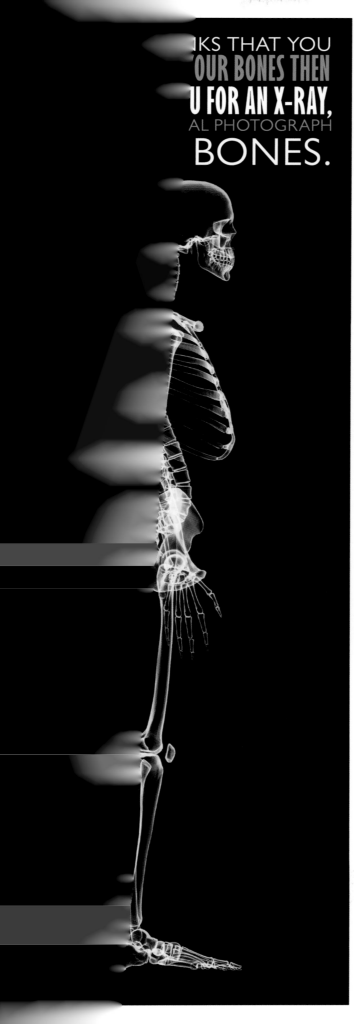

IKS THAT YOU
'OUR BONES THEN
U FOR AN X-RAY,
AL PHOTOGRAPH
BONES.

THE RIBS

Ribs act as a cage around your chest so that your **VITAL** organs are protected. You should be able to feel them under your skin. Ribs come in pairs. Most people have 12 pairs of ribs, but it is possible to be born with more or less.

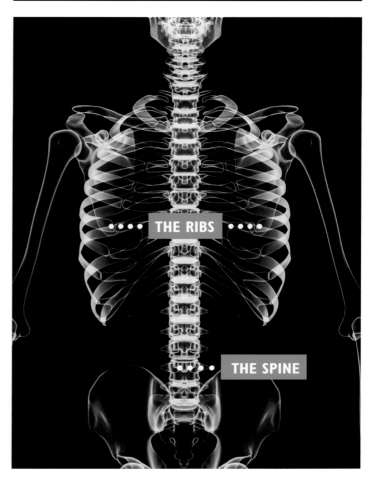

THE RIBS

THE SPINE

THE SPINE

The spine is located in the back and is the central pillar in the human skeleton. It is made up of 26 small bones called vertebrae. The top vertebrae are there to support the head as it is rather heavy. The bottom vertebrae are there to help you to carry weight and are also good for balance. The middle vertebrae help us to move. In between the vertebrae are disks which stop the bones from rubbing together. They also act as a cushion when we run or jump.

THE *Muscles*

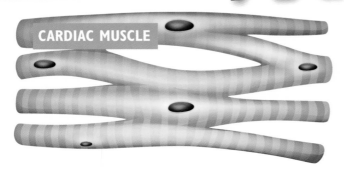

CARDIAC MUSCLE

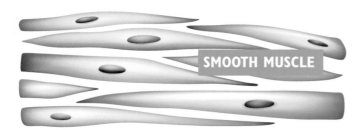

SMOOTH MUSCLE

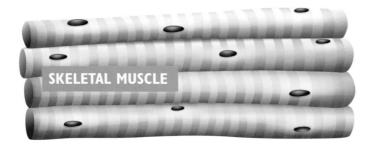

SKELETAL MUSCLE

WHAT ARE THEY FOR?

MUSCLES cover the human body and give it shape. They are attached to the skeleton and are able to move it by contracting and pulling on the bones. Muscles that are used a lot become bigger and stronger, whereas muscles that are not used can become weak.

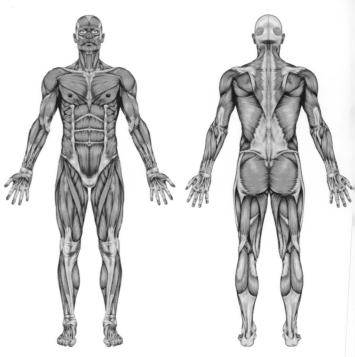

HOW MANY DO WE HAVE?

There are about 640 muscles in the human body. The most important muscle is the heart (see pages 10-11). There are three types of muscles: skeletal, smooth and cardiac. A skeletal muscle is one that is attached to the skeleton and helps us to move. Smooth muscles are found inside organs, such as the muscles in the stomach. We have no control over smooth muscles. The cardiac muscles are all linked to the heart.

THERE ARE ABOUT 30 MUSCLES IN THE HUMAN FACE. THESE MUSCLES ARE NEEDED FOR SMILING, FROWNING AND CHEWING, AMONGST OTHER THINGS.

MOVING

The skeletal muscles allow us to move our bodies. Even the smallest of movements, such as a nod or a blink, requires some muscles to work. Many muscles are arranged in pairs. When one of them contracts (shortens) the other relaxes and **VICE VERSA**. This is necessary because muscles can only pull bone; they cannot push. This allows movement to be made in both directions.

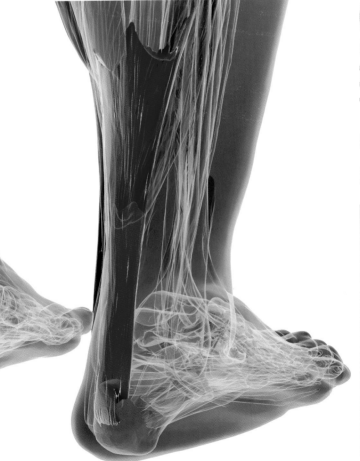

OUR HANDS ARE ABLE TO MOVE IN MANY DIFFERENT WAYS. AROUND 30 MUSCLES CONTROL THE HANDS; MOST OF THEM ARE ACTUALLY LOCATED IN OUR FOREARMS AND ARE ATTACHED TO THE HAND BY LONG TENDONS.

TENDONS

Muscles are attached to bones by connective tissues called tendons. Tendons are made out of strong fibres. The thickest tendon in the human body is the Achilles tendon, which is also known as the calcaneal tendon. It is located in the heel. It is possible to damage both your muscles and your tendons (both of which can be very painful). Muscles and tendons can often heal themselves if left to rest.

THE *Senses*

FIVE SENSES

HUMANS are considered to have five main senses – sight, touch, smell, taste and hearing. These senses are essential for our survival as they let us interact with what's around us and make it possible for us to be aware of danger. Some people do not have all of these five main senses, however many of thses people are able to continue living normal and happy lives. Part of the reason for this is because when someone loses one of their senses, their other senses can become **HEIGHTENED** in order to **COMPENSATE** for what has been lost.

EYELIDS ARE THERE TO PROTECT THE EYES. THEY WASH THEM WITH TEARS EVERY TIME THAT WE BLINK TO KEEP THEM FREE OF DUST AND GERMS

SEEING

Sight is the **DOMINANT** sense in humans. Our eyes are the organs that we use to see. Our eyes contain a lens that focuses light onto special sensors in the back of the eye. These sensors send signals to the brain about how much light and what colour light has entered the eye. Here, these signals are interpreted by the brain and are **CONVERTED** into the images we see.

HEARING

We use our ears to hear what is happening around us and to collect a great deal of information. Human ears can **DECIPHER** the cause, direction and nature of a sound and send messages to the brain **CONVEYING** this information. Humans can hear quite a range of sounds, although many animals can hear more.

EARS ALSO PLAY AN IMPORTANT ROLE IN BALANCE.

OUR NOSTRILS ARE LINED WITH SMALL HAIRS TO STOP DUST AND MOISTURE ENTERING OUR BODIES THROUGH OUR NOSES.

SMELLING

The nose contains special **RECEPTORS** that pick up odour from the air. We use our smell to entice our bodies to eat food. In fact, saliva in our mouths starts to flow before we've even put food into it, because of smell. The sense of smell is important in detecting danger, it can smell smoke if there is a fire or can smell whether a food has started to rot and is no good to eat.

TASTING

Smelling and tasting are closely linked. Smell receptors are far more powerful than taste receptors, however, which is why we sometimes cannot taste our food when we have a blocked nose. Taste receptors are located on our tongues. They help us to enjoy food and drink.

THERE ARE AROUND
10,000 TASTE BUDS
ON THE TONGUE.

TOUCHING

Our skin is the organ which provides us with the sense of touch. It is the only sense organ that has more than one role (see pages 22 & 23). The skin on different areas of the body has differing levels of sensitivity to touch and pressure. The hands, lips and tongue are the most sensitive areas.

Glossary

cease	stop
cholesterol	a type of fat found in blood
churn	mix around
compensate	make up for
converted	changed into
conveying	making something known and understood
decipher	work out
diameter	the distance through the centre of an object
dominant	strongest
elasticated	stretchy
follicles	hollow structure
generated	made
heightened	become more intense
informed choices	knowing all the options before you make a choice
isolation	being separated and alone
pigment	natural colouring
proteins	organic compounds that perform lots of very important roles in the body
receptors	receivers
subconsciously	without thought or intention
vessels	hollow containers
vice versa	the other way around
vital	needed

Index

appendix 21

bladder 20

bones 24-26

brain 8-9, 18, 20, 28-29

gall bladder 21

heart 10-12, 18, 26

kidneys 18, 20

large intestines 17, 21

liver 16, 18-19

lungs 10, 12-13

muscles 10, 13, 15-16, 26-27

nerves 8

oesophagus 15

pancreas 16, 21

pulse 11

ribs 12, 25

senses 7, 14, 22, 28-30

skeleton 7, 12, 24-26

skin 15, 22-23, 25, 30

small intestines 16-17

spine 25

stomach 15-16, 21, 26

teeth 15

tendons 27

PHOTO CREDITS

Photocredits: Abbreviations: l–left, r–right, b–bottom, t–top, c–centre, m–middle. All images are courtesy of Shutterstock.com.
2 – Syda Productions. 4-5m – jordache. 4ml – www.BillionPhotos.com. 4br – Duplass. 5tr – amenic181. 5br – pathdoc. 6ml – Monkey Business Images. 6br – Nerthuz . 7ml – Rawpixel.com. 7mr – Konstantin Shevtsov .8m – Sergey Nivens. 8bl – Sebastian Kaulitzki. 9r – Catalin Petolea. 10t – Mopic. 10br – PavloArt Studio. 11t – Gorosi. 11br – spass. 12tl – Sebastian Kaulitzki. 13l – Alex Mit. 13br – u3d. 14tr – Pressmaster. 15b – manas_ko. 16m – Sebastian Kaulitzki. 17mr – Sebastian Kaulitzki. 18-19m – decade3d – anatomy online. 19mr – Nerthuz. 20m – shutterstock_256695604.jpg. 21t – decade3d – anatomy online. 21b – Nerthuz. 22t – Creations. 23mr – Rawpixel.com. 23bl – Mega Pixel. 24-25 – yodiyim. 26tl – BlueRingMedia. 26mr – stihii. 27tr – Evgeny Bakharev. 27bl – goa novi. 28bl – Pressmaster. 28mr – Evgeny Atamanenko. 29ml – Rohappy. 29mr – anyaivanova. 30ml – Tatyana Vyc. 30mr – Alinute Silzeviciute. 31br – amenic181.
Images are courtesy of Shutterstock.com. With thanks to Getty Images, Thinkstock Photo and iStockphoto.